Setting up an out-of-school club

| L° °N TIME | STOCK NO.

Setting up an out-of-school club
Suzanne Brown

QUESTIONS
PUBLISHING
COMPANY

First published in 2000
by the Questions Publishing Company
27 Frederick Street, Birmingham B1 3HH

Designed by Al Stewart
Cover design by Sharonjit Samrai/Andrew Cottle

ISBN 1-84190-012-5

Contents

Section 1
Club Management

CHAPTER 1

Why bother?

The benefits to schools of setting up an out-of-school club

You may be a headteacher, senior manager or class teacher. You may have been tempted by the recent publicity about setting up out-of-school clubs. You may believe that helping parents by providing reliable, affordable, stimulating childcare around the school day is a good idea. Your education authority might agree with you.

What then?

It is one thing to subscribe to the concept but another to take the initiative and embark on what is, after all, peripheral to your core job as an educator. No one who is considering branching into school club provision should do so under the impression that it is easy.

If your school is situated in an area of relative prosperity where parents can afford to pay higher fees, you will find it less of a struggle. It will be easier still if the potential is such that a childcare business is prepared to take on the task on a profit-making basis. In this case you will have much less day-to-day responsibility and your share of the burden will be light.

However, if you are in an area where parents are not as wealthy, where many families depend upon a single parent or are experiencing crises of one kind or another and the potential for profit is minimal, then you may find yourself faced with a decision. Should you take the lead, forge ahead and accept the additional responsibilities, or should you leave it for another day?

The purpose of this book is to help those schools which are interested in setting up out-of-school provision but which are left to take the initiative themselves. It aims to give the school perspective and help by providing advice and proformas for those wading through bureaucracy and regulations.

If you have read this far and are still interested, then do be encouraged. Although it is time-consuming, initiating a club is extremely worthwhile. There are many benefits and they include:

- providing a safe environment for children who otherwise might have been left to their own devices at home;

- opportunities for children to mix with others of different ages;
- support for parents through providing childcare and increasing opportunities for them to take up work;
- providing respite for families in difficulty;
- increasing links between the school and the community;
- making better use of the school building and facilities;
- providing work opportunities for local adults;
- providing training opportunities for staff;
- attracting funding for resources for which you might otherwise not be eligible;
- attracting new parents who need childcare;
- raising the profile of the school with additional publicity;
- demonstrating that you respond to the needs of your community;
- developing an ethos of taking care of the 'whole child';
- improved communication between families and school;
- reduction in vandalism during the school holidays;
- easier access to school buildings for staff during the school holidays;
- placement for children left at school or who are collected late.

The list could continue and your own circumstances might reveal a wealth of additional benefits. You will need to keep these benefits and reasons for establishing a club at hand for those times when both you and others will query 'is it worth it?'

However, with commitment and determination and sound preparation, setting up an out-of-school club can be one of the most rewarding of initiatives. If you do take the lead, good luck and read on!

> "It was a wonderful feeling. Entering the school during the summer holidays, seeing the children sat eating their lunch. Such a variety of age groups from a variety of schools, talking, making friends, just like an extended family. The year before, the school was empty at this time. Now it's home to 32 children who love every minute of it."
>
> *Kids' club coordinator, Midlands*

Chapter 2

Assessing need

Do parents want a kids' club? What else is available locally? What kind of kids' club would they like?

Once you are convinced that establishing an out-of-school facility is a good idea, you need to check that others feel the same. Consider:

- Is there a need for the facility locally?
- Are there sufficient families in the area with young children?
- What childcare arrangements are they using at present?
- What childcare is available in the area?
- Is there a gap which your potential provision could fill?

You will need to spend time finding out about the childcare needs of your catchment and the provision that they have access to at present. Consider:

- What type of competition is there locally?
- What do they charge?
- When are they open?
- Who is using them at present?
- Are they full? Is there a waiting list for places?

You should spend time visiting other providers and, where possible, talking to coordinators and parents who are already using them. Social services will have a list of local registered provision, and there may be an early years development officer in your education authority who can also provide an overview.

This careful preparation will not only help you to determine whether it is worth opening a club or not, but will also provide you with local contacts and advice.

You should conduct a survey of your parents at an early stage. You will need to ask them whether they would use such a facility and also establish what type of service they require. The information you need falls under a number of headings:

Age range

What age group will you cater for? Possible ranges are:

- nursery age
- infant age
- junior age
- secondary age

Which category you choose will determine the type of registration you will need to undertake. There are far more stringent registration requirements for younger children. Catering for children under four-years-old will mean higher levels of staffing and additional space requirements. Provision for children aged four to eight years will also require registration but with higher child:playworker ratios and less space necessary. Catering only for children over the age of eight years will mean that you do not officially have to register your facilities.

Of course, the age you focus upon will largely depend on your school type, but even if you are a junior or middle school you may wish to include the whole primary age range in order to be of full benefit to your parents. However, this will mean you will have to consider how children will be transported to and from their infant schools.

Even if you begin by catering for children of primary age, you may find that as they move to secondary school you still receive requests for them to continue at the club. Will you continue to accept them? At what age will you draw the line? Some clubs have found it so difficult to turn children away once they transfer, that they have started new categories of participants such as volunteer helpers or 'trainees', thus giving older children minor responsibilities in order to involve them more.

The wider the age group you are catering for, the more difficult it can be to equip your facility, but the more convenient it will be for parents.

Opening hours

What will your opening hours be? The most common practice is to open from 8.00 a.m. to the beginning of school and from the end of the school day to 5.30 or 6.00 p.m. School holidays usually keep to the same opening times but continue through the normal school day, i.e. 8.00 a.m. – 6.00 p.m.

You will need to consider whether you wish to start both sessional and holiday-club care at the same time, or whether you wish to begin with sessions only and gradually extend your club to holiday periods too.

Be aware that an out-of-school facility takes time to grow. Opening up just before the long summer holiday will leave you vulnerable to large losses as you are unlikely to fill up immediately. Holiday periods require more staff and absorb more resources. The best holidays to start with are the October and February half-terms, when parents are less likely to take holidays for themselves and you will have a short period of time to 'test the water'.

In some schools, 'before-school' is not as popular. This often depends upon the time school starts. You may need to target your before-school club differently, e.g. by highlighting breakfast provision and opening it to a wider group of customers.

Charges

How much you charge will depend upon the type of catchment area you serve. Be aware not only of what parents can afford but also what other facilities charge. As an example, a sample charging policy for a West Midlands facility in an inner-city environment can be found in Appendix A of this book.

When determining your charging policy, you will need to decide whether to offer different rates depending upon family income and/or the number of children in a family using the facility. Some kind of sliding scale is usually adopted, but this does make working out the bills more difficult!

Payment methods

How will people pay and how flexible will your arrangements for payment be? Will you require payment in advance, weekly, monthly or daily?

It is likely that you will wish to be as accommodating as possible. For some parents it is preferable to pay by cheque on a monthly basis, whereas others prefer to pay as they use. More flexible arrangements make it more difficult to keep track of who owes what, but people will be grateful for them.

Who can join?

Will the club only be open for children at your school or to all children locally? If you extend the facility to other schools, you will need to decide about transportation and make arrangements for collection and drop-off.

Holiday times are less of a problem, and certainly in the early days you are likely to need to open your facility to the whole community, not just children at your school. You should determine your admissions criteria at an early stage. It might be 'first come, first served' or preference given to children on site. Whatever decision you make, you should implement it fairly and consistently.

Help and advice

Is there anyone available who can help you make these decisions? You should look to several different sources for initial advice. Consult with:

- parents (see Appendix B for a sample questionnaire);
- other local clubs;
- feeder schools/other local schools;
- day-care advisor (social services);
- your local branch of Kids' Club Network;
- your local education authority – some LEAs now have appointed people responsible for overseeing the development of this kind of facility.

In addition, there may be other local groups such as community action groups who can provide guidance or suggestions.

Collect in your impressions, meet with representatives and distribute and analyse questionnaires. Look at the results and then share your findings with others in the school. However, be warned: parents tend to answer on a 'just in case' basis. You will probably find that a significant number of respondents would like to see a club in operation but may not intend to use it straight away.

> "At first we were very excited to see such a range of positive responses. There was no doubt that parents wanted a club. However, when it came to opening, many of the parents contacted were still hanging on to original arrangements whilst they saw how it went. This was really frustrating. Fortunately, the grants helped us to keep going until parents felt confident enough to say – 'Right, we'll give it a try!'"
> *Primary school headteacher*

CHAPTER **3**

The management committee

Who should be on our committee? How often should it meet? What is a constitution? Who does the work?

You have some ideas, you have researched your provision and can begin to see what your club might look like. Now you need to share the burden of the next stage of implementation. You need to identify a management committee.

You will need other people to help take responsibility for the club, both in terms of management responsibility and advice, and also moral support during the more difficult times. A management committee is the usual route for enabling this.

Ideally your committee should comprise:

- a member of the local community
- a parent
- another senior manager within the school
- a home/school liaison representative
- a member of your governing body
- a financial advisor/administrator
- a representative playworker
- the coordinator of the club

Initially you will be unable to include your club coordinator or playworker staff but you may wish to consider inviting them to be members once they are recruited.

The suggested list of members is not easy to create in reality. People will need to give their time on a voluntary basis and be accessible for meetings, and many of the people who are eligible may already be overburdened with voluntary activities. However, don't be daunted. Bear in mind that you might be able to combine roles. For example:

- a parent is a member of the local community;
- your senior manager may also have responsibility for home/school liaison;
- your governor may be a parent and will generally be a member of the local community.

As long as you have two or three additional members who are prepared to meet on a half-termly basis, you will have a 'skeleton crew' for your initiative. As the club grows and staff are recruited, you may be able to increase the number and develop a more representative body.

Establishing your committee

As you become more established you will need to have a constitution for your club (see example Appendix C). In the early stages don't worry too much about this but do begin to establish rules for meetings and the roles that each of you will take. You will need to decide:

1. Who will be the chair?
2. How the agenda will be set?
3. Who will take the minutes?
4. Who will take the responsibility for:

   - administration?
   - producing documents?
   - liasing with social services?
   - applying for grants and funding?
   - interviewing and appointing staff?

Remember, the purpose of your committee is to determine the strategic direction of your club, monitor its performance and keep looking ahead to the next stages of its development. At this stage, you should, between you, agree an action plan to take you forward. As your club and your committee develop, you will need to produce a business plan, which will give you a set of targets on an annual basis.

As the club builds, each meeting should include:

- a review of the club on a termly basis;
- a financial update;
- a personnel update;
- a review of training;
- plans for the following term/holiday;
- a review of overall progress using the action plan/business plan as a benchmark;
- focus on an area of policy for either preparation or review.

The first meeting

At your first meeting you will want to make some decisions about the nature of your club and how to proceed. With the information you have gathered in front of you, you will want to make some concrete and some tentative decisions, as shown in Figure 1.

Figure I

Core decisions	Age range
	Opening times
	Aims and objectives
	Admissions policy
	Implementation plan
	Site of the club
	Registration number
	Club fees
	Sources of funding
Tentative decisions (will need some further consideration/ advice)	Methods of publicity
	Appointment of staff
	Staff rotas
	Activities and planning format
	Documents and policies
Other agencies to consult	Social services
	Governing body
	Out-of-school development officer
	School staff
	Cleaners and caretaker
	Other local clubs

Involving school staff

Although the management committee will have the strategic overview of the club, as a school-based initiative it is very important to 'take the school with you'. There will be members of school staff who have concerns about out-of-school provision and it may be that their objections could become detrimental to the club if they are not carefully managed. You will need to involve:

The caretaker

Your school caretaker needs to be consulted about the opening/ closing arrangements and about any effect your club will have on procedures for cleaning and management of the school premises.

Do emphasise that other clubs have found that opening their doors out-of-school hours has reduced vandalism.

Teaching staff

They may be affected, depending upon the nature of your premises. If any of their normal teaching areas will be used in any way, consultation and discussion should begin as soon as possible. Don't wait for a problem to emerge.

Emphasise the benefits of the club (see Chapter 1) and how children remaining behind at the end of the day will be able to be accommodated there in cases of emergency, etc.

Depending upon the age profile of your staff, you may wish to offer different rates for their own children to attend the club.

The governing body

As they have responsibility for the school premises and activities that are conducted there, the governing body should be consulted and bulletined at each governing body meeting. They will need copies of the business plan and, of course, will need to agree the principles and decisions of the management committee for the club to go ahead.

You may find the reaction of governors to be mixed, so have your reasons for what you are doing ready at your fingertips. If possible, invite someone else (ideally from another governing body) who has had experience of setting up a school club and can speak from experience. If there is resistance, it might be that a representative from the governing body could accompany you on a visit to another local club in order to see one in action and to talk to the organisers.

Frequency of meetings

How often you meet may vary according to the stage of implementation you have reached. During the initial phase you may need to meet every two to three weeks. Once your club is established, then an average schedule would include half-termly meetings.

If you find that the agenda becomes too long and unmanageable, you may decide to hold more meetings or elect to have sub-committees and/or working parties to deal with specific aspects of the club or areas for development. Don't make the meetings so long-winded that your volunteers lose their enthusiasm and become non-attenders.

The constitution

The constitution is an agreed set of procedures for how your committee operates. It helps to define the status of your club and clarifies how major decisions affecting its future will be determined. The constitution should include:

- the date the constitution was adopted;
- the objectives of the club;
- procedures for dealing with receipts and expenditures;
- accounting procedures;
- how the constitution can be altered;
- what its powers are;
- the voting arrangements;
- the names or representations of committee members;
- the roles of different committee members;
- what will happen if the organisation should be dissolved;
- how committee members are to be elected and removed.

The constitution should be signed by all the committee members. A sample constitution can be found in Appendix C.

> "At first there was great reluctance from the caretaker and cleaning staff. They could only see that it would mean more work. In fact, the playworkers have taken a lot of the responsibility for keeping the club tidy and the caretaker is thrilled that the number of incidents of vandalism seem to have reduced. We can only think that having lots of people around during the holidays has prevented the intrusions we used to suffer from before. He's all for the club now!"
> *Headteacher, Junior School*

CHAPTER 4
Writing a business plan
Setting the framework for your initiative

The business plan is the central steering document for your club. It should be discussed and drafted with the management committee, and is a public document which you will require for grant applications.

Reviewed annually, the business plan represents a balance between the description of current provision and targets for the coming year. You will have already decided some of its content during the early stages of the club's development; other areas will need consultation and will result in policy formation.

Although it is initially hard work, you will find that much of the plan's content will be transferable to other documents you draft, e.g. your staff handbook and introductory information for parents. It is therefore worthwhile taking the time to ensure that its content is agreed, cohesive and comprehensive.

You may wish to make review and discussion of different sections a regular part of your management committee meetings. There is a sample business plan in Appendix G of this book. Obviously, different clubs will place different emphases, but generally the plan should include:

1. Aims

What are the 'guiding principles' of your club? Depending upon the area you serve, built into your aims may be aspects of social regeneration and/or the enrichment of children's experiences through a defined list of extra-curricular activities. You may be working alongside other organisations whose aims you share, such as social services or community groups. You might wish to highlight the career opportunities that club provision enables, or the benefits to the school as well as its community.

2. Background information

The inclusion of a brief history of your club to date can be a useful reminder of just how much you have accomplished and the direction in which you are heading. You might also include here some summary information about the context or catchment of your club. It is useful to collect data and statistics that will help build a profile of the club as this can be used when applying for grants and subsidies. Information about the number of single parents, children from ethnic minority families and children from families living at or below the poverty line can usefully substantiate any claim that you make.

3. About the club

This section should include some basic information about how the club operates, e.g:

- current staff and staffing levels
- priorities for training
- premises
- opening times
- fees
- admissions policy
- refreshments policy
- activities available
- management committee
- involvement of parents

4. Financial information

You will need to include a cash flow forecast and financial targets. Your level of accuracy will depend upon the stage of implementation of your club, but you should aim to be as accurate as possible in order to demonstrate your long-term viability. You might also include details of arrangements for the auditing of your accounts and payment of staff salaries.

5. Plans for the club

This section will help steer your club through the next year. Areas to identify include:

- ways in which you will publicise your club;
- organisations to which you can apply for supplementary funding;
- targets linked to staff training and development;
- development of policies and procedures;
- monthly financial targets;
- long-term goals for the club.

6. Review date

Even within a year, a club can grow and develop at an astonishing rate. By that time, some targets and ambitions you began with may well have either been achieved or no longer seem relevant. The business plan should be a working document which needs regular amendment to keep it relevant, and its review provides an opportunity for discussion about the club's progress in general. Be prepared to consult and evaluate openly.

> "At first I thought that putting together a business plan was just a chore. The initial plan, however, involved us in lots of discussion that made us clarify the purpose and direction of the club. Now we refer to it as a central document and use it to help us monitor progress and evaluate performance on an annual basis."
>
> *Headteacher involved in establishing an out-of-school club*

CHAPTER 5

Applying for funding

Who to apply to, how to apply and what you will need to supply; fundraising events

One of the most time-consuming aspects of setting up a club is applying for grants. At the present time, no money is automatically available to help support club start-up and development. There is, however, a range of funding opportunities for which you will need to bid. Without access to these funds, you will find it very difficult to establish your club.

In some local authorities, guidance is available as to local businesses and particular, local projects and initiatives which might look favourably on an application. If your LEA has appointed an early years/childcare advisor, they will be able to provide you with this information and suggest the routes for accessing the guidance.

You need to apply for grants well in advance of needing them. The process is usually very long and the outcome tends to be delayed. You may need to wait until the appropriate panel meets to discuss your application, and the panel may then even defer a decision until it has received further information.

Look carefully at the guidelines for application. Check that you meet the criteria, and be rigorous about following the procedures and including the information they ask for. Errors will cost you time.

Sources of funding

There are various possible sources of funding:

The New Opportunities Fund

'Out-of-school hours' initiatives are at present one of the main areas for the allocation of funding from the New Opportunities Fund (NOF). Applications for under £50,000 are welcomed, especially if they include projects that link education and childcare. The NOF will allocate £220 million from the proceeds of the National Lottery to create out-of-school childcare places for 865,000 children across the UK by 2003.

To qualify for this, you will need to demonstrate either that you are offering new childcare places as part of a new project or that you are increasing your club size. The fund will provide money for:

- start-up costs;
- running costs for existing providers who wish to provide new places;
- small capital projects such as the purchase of equipment or refurbishment which will enable new places to be provided by either new or existing providers.

The NOF is looking for clubs that:

- have evidence of good quality childcare;
- have plans that fit in with local strategic planning;
- have plans that meet the needs of parents;
- have accessible provision;
- comply with relevant statutory obligations for working with children;
- have support from the local community;
- have added to existing provision;
- have viable plans for sustainability;
- offer value for money;
- demonstrate a commitment to equal opportunities.

It will take at least four months to assess an application. Maintenance funding is not part of the NOF's brief.

Regional advice is available and application forms can be obtained by calling one of the following numbers:

England:	0845-604 0555
Scotland:	0845-606 1199
Wales:	0845-606 4567
Northern Ireland:	0845-600 4848

The application form has been reduced in complexity from earlier grant forms but will take someone a significant chunk of time. If at all possible, delegate this responsibility. As well as the actual form to complete, you will need to attach:

- a bank statement
- a copy of your registration document (if you have one)
- your constitution
- your accounts

Local Authorities

Until recently, TECs held money for the start-up and growth of out-of-school clubs. However, this responsibility has now moved to local authorities, who may well have appointed staff specifically to allocate funding. As well as money for start-up projects, there is an allocation for the maintenance of existing clubs. Money for 'sustaining good quality childcare provision' is particularly useful in those cases where a club is already established but is not yet breaking even.

Subsidised places will form part of the authority's childcare plans, and there may well be a priority list linked to catchment and targeted zones of disadvantage. The amount of funding available through this source is much smaller than the NOF funding, but has the advantage of not requiring you to grow. The applications are also usually more user-friendly and require less paperwork.

It is likely, however, that you will still need to provide evidence of your accounts and the long-term financial viability of your club.

Education Extra

Education Extra is a national organisation which has traditionally encouraged extra-curricular activities. It is much more focused upon school-based initiatives and has become very much involved with the development of homework clubs and other out-of-schools learning opportunities.

It invites applications for small grants for initiatives which require capital costs and are part of a proposed programme. It also allocates certification for schemes, and encourages publicity and media attention.

You will need to join Education Extra to receive their newsletter and to be eligible to apply for a grant. They also publish some very useful materials about running extra-curricular activities, usually with a more educational slant. The amount available is very limited and can be used to help boost additional resources, but it cannot be used to support running costs.

For more information about the application procedure contact:
  Education Extra
  St Margaret's House
  17 Old Ford Road
  London E2 9PL
  Tel: 020 8983 1061

Company support and sponsorship

You might find support from companies who have:

- employees using your facilities;
- local business which they would like to promote;
- an interest in raising their profile in the local community and making a 'community-friendly' name for themselves.

Although not all companies might be willing or able to supply large grants, there are other ways in which they can be asked to help. For example:

- sponsoring a particular place for a child – either someone who is working for them or a child in need;
- donating unwanted items of furniture or other goods;
- providing advice or support, e.g. help with an audit or publication of a leaflet;
- allowing publicity for the club in their staffroom/shop floor/ waiting rooms, etc;
- providing sufficient money for a particular project to take place, e.g. a trip out or a visiting artist.

Vague requests for support are unlikely to be successful: you are more likely to receive support if you are able to approach a named person with a specific project. A carefully thought through idea which will address some of their objectives as well as your own is far more likely to be fruitful.

Advice on applications

On your applications do remember to do the following:

- Target your applications carefully: it can be a time-consuming process, so make sure you fit the criteria for grants before you apply.
- Find out as much as you can about the organisation you are applying to and the type of bid they are likely to look favourably on. Are they prepared to give grants towards running costs or just capital items? Do they have a particular interest in community development or educational projects?
- Whatever the organisation's main interests, tailor your request accordingly.
- Seek advice from community action groups, your local education authority and other clubs. Who do they know about? Who have they been successful with?
- Copy any application you make – some of the information you need to produce will need to be repeated on other forms.

- Try to share the burden of making your applications.
- Try to collect information to support your bids. Funding organisations are particularly interested in the number of single-parents using your facility, the number of people accessing employment or training through the start-up of your club, the number of ethnic minority families using your facility and the number of special needs children using your facility.

Organising events

You may decide to organise fundraising activities and events of your own. Some suggestions include:

- sponsored events, e.g. walks, bike rides, silences, snooker tournaments, etc.;
- autumn fairs – if not holding your own, you could involve children in making items to sell at your school's seasonal fair;
- taking part in a mail-order catalogue – especially in the run up to Christmas;
- social events to which adults and children are invited, e.g. fashion shows, line-dancing, bingo, roller-skating, etc.;
- raffles with prizes donated from local businesses;
- jumble sales, car boot and table-top sales.

Where possible, try to make the fundraising opportunity a social event too, e.g. by including a barbecue. Involve children and parents as much as possible in the planning of the event. Having a stake in the early stages will hopefully encourage a higher level of participation throughout.

It might be possible to combine an event with another local kids' club. Shared events can be exciting, providing opportunities not only for children to mix but for staff to discover and share new skills and ideas. This could be particularly useful where minority groups are under-represented in particular communities. Rural and urban clubs might share practice, and clubs with no ethnic mix would benefit from a day of greater cultural diversity.

> "I've found it quite time consuming applying for grants. However, our catchment is such that parents could not afford to pay the full cost of a childcare place. It's a relief to see that there is now money available for maintenance of existing provision. I just hope this will continue to be available as we are always going to need to subsidise our families."
>
> *Coordinator of an inner city kids' club*

Chapter 6

Social services registration

*Who to contact, what to expect,
regulations and guidance*

It is a legal requirement for your club to register under the Children's Act 1989. Do not expect this to be a straightforward process. One of the frustrations of establishing a club is that you will be dealing with the bureaucracy wielded by both the education authority and social services. Both have different requirements.

Your first point of contact is your day-care advisor, who will provide you with a list of regulations for your local authority. Authorities do differ on what they expect.

As an example of the kinds of regulations you are likely to meet, the following headings are taken from one local education authority's handbook on standards for day care:

Premises – size, location

Premises should be warm and well ventilated, welcoming and light. There should be easy and safe access for children or adults with a disability.

The local authority's planning, environmental health and fire departments will need to be consulted and their requirements complied with.

There should be 2.3 square metres (25 sq. ft) of clear floor space per child. No more than 26 children can be accommodated in one room, regardless of size.

The premises must be free from hazards and all reasonable steps must be taken to ensure a safe environment, i.e.

- all heaters must be safely guarded;
- all low-level glass should conform to British Standards;
- cleaning materials must be stored out of reach;
- there must be access to a telephone;
- a first aid kit must be provided, all treatment must be recorded and medicines must be stored out of the reach of children;
- there must be at least one member of staff who holds a current first aid certificate;

- consent to medical treatment in the case of an emergency.

Insurance requirements

The day care provider will need to possess public liability insurance.

Further advice

There may be further advice on:

- equal opportunities
- basic equipment needed
- working in partnership with parents
- child protection issues
- discipline

Any fee for registration to your club will vary depending upon whether your facilities are sessional (two to four hours a day) or open for more than four hours per sessions (holiday clubs). This is usually payable annually, as registration only covers a period of 12 months. Someone from the club will need to act as the 'registered person' who will be named on the certificate and will have overall responsibility for the appointment of staff, the maintenance of the premises and general policy.

Before you open your club you will need to ensure that all appointed staff have had police checks, and you will need to demonstrate that the range of qualifications and experience of the staff are adequate. This is especially difficult to ensure at present, as many potential staff will have one or the other but not both.

Once you have received your registration certificate you will still be open to intermittent checks and inspections, and you must ensure that any actions you are required to fulfil are carried through. You should display your certificate for parents to see, and keep a copy for your own reference. Many applications for funding require copies of your certificate.

Sessional care (term-time) and holiday care can be registered for separately. The checks and requirements for holiday care are usually more stringent due to the full-time nature of the provision.

You may discover that there are anomalies between what is expected in the kids' club and what is allowed in school, e.g. provision of liquid soap, storage of perishables from sandwich boxes, etc. But stick with it – it's worth it in the end.

"We have found the process of registration quite frustrating. There are several differences between education authority requirements and social services requirements. For example, we can use bars of soap in school but need liquid soap in the kids' club. At present, however, there is no way around the red tape. You hope for a supportive and sympathetic childcare advisor and do your best to meet the demands of registration."

Coordinator of an expanding kids' club

Chapter 7

Appointing and developing your staff

The selection process – advertising and interviewing; training and developing your staff to create a well-qualified team

Staff recruitment is one of the most crucial and most difficult aspects of setting up a club. The nature of childcare and the present funding arrangements mean that staff salaries are generally limited. Depending upon where your club is based, you may find it hard to offer anything other than a minimum wage to staff, if your costs to parents are also to be contained.

Good quality childcare requires a well-qualified, experienced staff who are paid a salary which appropriately reflects the importance of their role and the responsibility that it carries. Attracting this workforce and findings the funds to pay them is not easy, not least because the working hours are those when many people wish to be at home themselves to cater for their own families. You will have to work hard to get and to retain the right people.

In the initial stages you will need to do the following:

1. Check what the usual rates of pay are for your area. You will need to have two pay scales to start with – one for playworkers and one for your coordinator. Remember that you will need to add National Insurance contributions to the total salary figure.

2. Look at your present staff in school. Working in a kids' club can sometimes be of interest to midday supervisors and other part-time ancillary staff.

3. Advertise your positions locally in good time. You might want to place the job advertisements in:

- local shops and/or post offices
- parents' room/other local schools
- your local newspaper
- the jobcentre
- local training colleges/universities

4. Prepare your job description, person specification and application

form (samples of these can be found in Appendix M of this book). You should demonstrate a fair appointments process in a similar way to school appointments. Decide exactly what kind of person you are looking for and the skills they will require.

5. Set a final date for applications, a date for shortlisting and a date for interview.

Remember to allow enough time to take up references and for social services to carry out their police and health checks.

The advertisement

When drafting out your advertisement, keep in mind the kind of person you are hoping to attract. Where are they likely to look for information about available posts? What basic information will they need to know to encourage them to find out more? Have you included the main points in an easily accessible and attractive form?

Your advertisement should include:

- the organisation's name
- address and contact details
- the purpose of the organisation
- main points from the job description and person specification
- pay rates
- how to find out more – contact numbers etc.

Person specification and job description

You need to spend time deciding what the main jobs for your playworkers will be and how they will fit into the team. At all stages of the recruitment process, you must bear in mind the relationships, roles and strengths of those already working for you.

Decide what your priorities for recruitment are. Organise them into 'desirable' and 'essential' qualities. Are you more anxious to have someone who is keen and willing to learn or someone who already has a good, solid foundation of previous experience? You may have to compromise on some of your desirables, but you should remain firm on those characteristics you consider essential.

The following headings might be useful for you to consider:

- health and physical characteristics
- qualifications
- work experience and achievements
- special skills

- interests
- personality
- personal circumstances

Many of your applicants will have a range of commitments and current working patterns that will mean you must carefully consider:

- Your policy on workers' own children – are they allowed in the club?
- Flexibility in arranging rotas.

For the job description you will have to consider:

- what proportion of playworkers' time will be allocated to preparation, tidying up and meetings;
- whether playworkers will be required to be part of the management committee;
- the role of the coordinator in building up the team and how this is to be encouraged;
- how you will develop your personnel and when their performance might be reviewed;
- what your policy is on covering for absent staff and for time off for holidays;
- the skills and strengths of existing team members and where any gaps in expertise may be.

Key headings for the job description include:

- Job title
- Name
- Reporting to
- Responsible for
- Purpose of job
- Key responsibilities
- Additional responsibilities

You may wish to appoint not only permanent members of staff but one or two casual playworkers (who may have been unsuccessful candidates at interview). These can be asked at an early stage if they would be prepared to take on casual work, and can be police checked in preparation.

Always try to have at least one person as a back-up to your arrangements.

The application form

You may wish to use one of the following:

- a standard application form already issued from the school for the appointment of other school staff;
- an adapted version containing the club's logo and with some questions removed/added;
- a specially created application form that takes account of the particular requirements of school club posts.

Which ever you choose, give careful consideration at the start to the form you would like.

On your application form make sure you include questions relating to:

- qualifications and experience
- current employer and previous employers
- name, address and referees
- opportunity for candidates to include more information about themselves and their suitability for the post

Shortlisting

Ideally involve your interviewing panel in the shortlisting process. That way they will be aware of the factors already considered and what your priorities are.

Keep the job description and person specification close to you during shortlisting and refer to them frequently. They should help you to make any difficult decisions. You will need to consider the weight you will give to the presentation of application. You may well feel that someone who cannot be bothered to present themselves reasonably well in a written form is unsuitable for the post. However, in some cases you may decide to place less emphasis upon written skills and prefer to speak to possible candidates over the phone.

Let people know as soon as possible the date and time of their interview and if there will be an opportunity to look around first. You will also need to send off for references and copy applications for the interview itself.

You may decide at this point to set the questions for the interview and decide who will ask what.

Equal opportunities

Be careful to ensure that your selection process is fair. You should not discriminate on the grounds of gender, disability or ethnic and cultural group.

All candidates should be treated in the same way and be asked the same core questions. Ideally, include a balance of representative interviewers if this is possible. It is good practice to keep copies of application forms and notes made during the interview, just in case a candidate should question your decision at a later stage. It is surprising how quickly one interview erases the memory of those before.

Developing your staff

Finding the right staff with sufficient qualifications and experience is a very difficult task. Training and development of the staff you recruit will be a priority. There are several ways in which you can do this:

NVQs

There is now an NVQ in playwork which is specifically aimed at out-of-school club playworkers. As with other NVQs, it consists of a range of units with lists of criteria to help the assessor decide whether a candidate is sufficiently competent.

Level 2 of the NVQ is aimed at playworkers, and level 3 at playworkers with more responsibility – possibly in a coordinating role. Interested candidates should register first with a local college. They will then need to find an assessor; the college should be able to help with this. At a later stage you may wish to encourage one of your staff to become an assessor, as having an in-house assessor cuts down the cost of the NVQ and is generally more convenient.

Once registered, candidates begin to collect together a portfolio of evidence to demonstrate their competence. This can include photographs, samples of completed work, examples of policies and procedures, witness testimonies and written assignments. The candidate will need to be observed by the assessor and provided with regular feedback.

In some cases, a gap in knowledge or skill may be identified by the assessor and the candidate may need to attend a course to fill this gap. In many areas, courses are now running which aim to provide all the underpinning knowledge for the playwork NVQ. These courses require a more hefty commitment. Other useful courses would include:

- first aid
- health and safety
- equal opportunities
- child protection
- food and hygiene
- activity planning

For the club coordinator, depending upon the level of responsibility required, a business skills course might also be useful.

The NVQ has the advantage of acknowledging any previous achievements of the candidate (e.g. certificates and modules already obtained can be used as evidence). It is, however, quite time consuming to put together the portfolios, and the language and presentation can be confusing.

In-house development

On occasion it may be that several members of staff are in need of training in a particular area. Every playworker should have some knowledge of first aid and it may be that the easiest way of securing this is to arrange a special training course on site.

Although it is likely you would have to pay for this, there are other areas of training which might be provided, either by a member of the school staff or someone on the team. Sharing expertise will be as essential and cost effective in the school club as in school generally.

Some club staff meetings and/or management committee meetings should include discussion of policies and issues. You might want to place each of your policies regularly on the agenda to examine some of their practical implications.

Annual review and development meetings

Each member of your school club staff should be entitled to an annual discussion about their progress and development needs. You will need to decide how formal this should be. Some staff will not be used to such attention and will find it very difficult to contribute positively to a highly structured meeting. Others will benefit from having a framework of questions and headings to assess their progress against.

In Appendix Q there is a sample of a relatively informal proforma which might be the focus of your discussion. It is, of course, important that any needs identified are acted upon and that the discussions remain confidential. Many staff will find it useful to take this opportunity to air grievances. This is an important benefit of the process.

You will need to decide who conducts the meetings. You might decide to do it yourself or allocate the responsibility to the club coordinator. Much will depend upon the personality and ability of your coordinator and his/her relationship with staff. An alternative is to give people the option.

You will need to meet with the coordinator yourself. The coordinator will need to reflect on his/her own development needs and those of the team.

You should make evaluation of the club and staff comments part of the club ethos. Playworkers will have significant contributions to make to documents, business plans and target setting. Do consult and make use of the variety of opinions you will encounter. The stake that consultation gives people is often very productive in terms of their motivation and willingness to implement orders.

Visiting other clubs

If you are able, encourage staff to visit other clubs and observe how they operate. Before they go, discuss with them a list of questions or points to look out for. A focused visit is usually most productive.

Consider:

- What do you feel you need to improve?
- What questions might you ask at a neighbouring club to help you address this?
- What will you be looking out for?
- How will you feed this back to other members of staff?
- How will you evaluate the success of your visit?

If more than one playworker makes a visit, it might be feasible to target different areas of the club for observation. Do share the purpose of your visit with the host club, and be considerate as to preventing any disruption and issues of confidentiality.

If you build up a strong local network, it might be possible for clubs to share in-house training and arrange more frequent staff swaps.

Keep a record of the qualifications and courses attended by staff. This will be useful if you should embark on a quality assurance scheme, and also for registration purposes. Certificates obtained by staff could be displayed in the club and photocopies kept in your club's own portfolio of achievements.

Do find time to reward and thank school club staff. Cards and small acknowledgements of the important role they take will be appreciated. They will become a team within your larger school framework and should be encouraged to adopt the usual staff outings, photographs and celebrations.

"It's been really gratifying to see how Christine has come on since she started working in the club. During her first months she really lacked confidence and needed a lot of support. I was worried initially about how she would cope with the mounting paperwork and administration demands. Now she has developed a whole range of systems of her own which have really superseded the original ones. I don't think she knew she had it in her!"

Deputy headteacher of a primary school

CHAPTER 8

Documentation

What you need to have in place; where it should be stored; the headings it should include

Your kids' club is no different from school in needing a variety of policy documents. Experience in preparing similar policies for the school as a whole makes this a familiar activity. In the school club context there is the advantage that consultation and discussion involves fewer individuals, and implementation is more straightforward and easier to monitor.

In some cases you will be able to use parts of your mainstream documentation (e.g. health and safety policy, child protection policy, equal opportunities policy). You will need to alter the job titles of people responsible, streamline and amend the line management responsibilities and adjust to suit the particular context of the club. You may, however, be able to keep to a similar format.

If possible, try to share the work of preparing these documents with your management committee. It is reasonable for one individual to prepare a draft, perhaps based on a policy model. This draft can then be discussed at the next committee meeting and (following alterations) implemented accordingly. This is one time when involving club staff on the committee will help avoid having to discuss the document in several different forums.

Do ensure that staff are aware of the implications for practice. If necessary, bullet-point the sections that have a direct relevance, or provide a summary sheet of 'what this means for you'. Set a review date for all your documents and stick to it. Even if nothing needs changing, it is a good opportunity to remind everyone of what is supposed to happen and to check that it *is* happening.

If possible, establish some ways of monitoring the implementation yourself, e.g. by collecting in the accident book at the end of the year, rewarding children receiving merit stickers, etc.

Training courses to support some of the procedures will be available locally. You will probably need to encourage staff to attend courses in health and safety, child protection, equal opportunities, etc. Attendance will help them to build an NVQ portfolio where this is appropriate.

Discuss where your documents should be stored. All documents should be easily accessible. Every member of staff should receive one on joining the club and be required to read and inwardly digest it. As you become more established and your list of documentation increases, a 'Have you read?' checklist can be useful as part of the staff information pamphlet.

Keep copies centrally. Registration information about the children should be kept easily to hand and stored safely but be quickly collectable in case of fire or emergency. As the size and range of your club increases, you may find that keeping a set of index cards with emergency information on is a more practical way of transporting essential information.

Information for parents should be given to all new parents registering their child. Many clubs ask parents to sign an acknowledgement slip after receiving this information to agree to the terms and condition. Alternatively this can be part of your registration pro forma.

All of the documents listed in Table 1 have proforma examples in the appendices to this book.

Document	Storage	Audience	Headings	Notes	Appendix
Equal opportunities policy	Every member of staff – one kept centrally	New staff	Aims Staff development Activities Admissions Resources Management Behaviour of children Monitoring and evaluation	You may need to involve staff in your own form of in-house training to supplement this. Although most aspects will be common sense, people involved in education can forget how some of the principles are less commonly acknowledged and agreed. Do talk it through and ensure that all staff are clear about their obligations.	L
Child protection guidelines	Every member of staff – one kept centrally	New staff	Rationale Responsibilities of playworkers Actions for playworkers Agencies to contact Keeping records Code of conduct	Once more, make sure staff are familiar with their responsibilities as outlined in the document. The essential inform-ation here is to record and refer. Some discussion of possible issues for your school and attention to sharing information about particular individuals may be necessary. Be aware, however, that some of your staff may also be parents with children at the school and will have additional roles and responsibilities. Sometimes this overlap can be useful in drawing together strands of information but do ensure staff are aware of the need to retain confidentiality and are sensitive to some of the information and issues they may have access to.	N

CHAPTER 9

Financial planning

Procedures you will need to have in place

If you are lucky, you will have a member of your management committee who is capable of taking on the administrative workload that accompanies setting up a club and who is prepared to do so. You should certainly make this a delegated role if at all possible, and you may need to employ someone or increase the hours of an office member of staff to cope with the additional work.

As a club grows, its turnover can become surprisingly large, especially when a holiday club is involved. You will need to set up procedures and checks to allow money to be collected and stored safely. There should be an in-built system of accountability and a procedure for paying staff promptly and appropriately.

You will need to have in place the following:

For staff salaries
- clarified hours of working and pay scale;
- time sheets to record hours worked;
- bank account to pay cheques and National Insurance contributions.

For income recording
- a method of recording what is owed against what is taken;
- a cash box and procedure for collecting and storing money;
- collection of money on a regular basis for safe banking.

For monitoring and forecasting
- a means of checking up and following up debts;
- a means of providing a running account of the club finances to help provide information for the cash-flow forecast;
- the involvement of an external body for the purpose of audit.

Do seek out advice on these from other local kids clubs and the Kids' Club Network. Different systems work for different people. In some authorities, the payment of club staff has been included within Local Management of Schools (LMS). You may decide to run your own payroll, but if so you will need someone who is in a position to take responsibility for this.

If you are open during the long summer holiday, you will need to make particular arrangements for the payment of staff.

You may wish to provide receipts for parents. These can be helpful, not only for the parents themselves, but for you to log outstanding monies.

Remember to keep detailed records of staff. You will need to inform the Inland Revenue as staff move on, and you will need to adjust your own records accordingly.

Organising insurance

There are some insurance firms who now specialise in insuring kids' clubs. Although some aspects of the club may be insured within your school insurance, it is wise to invest in additional insurance to make sure that you are covered for use of the school buildings outside normal school hours.

Moreton Michel Insurance have specifically targeted school clubs and offer a variety of packages. Their address can be found at the back of this book. Whichever scheme you choose, you will need to be insured for full public liability.

"To start with we had very little in the way of formal records and monitoring systems. We soon found, however, that the amount of money we were taking meant that we could no longer rely on a range of informal methods. We had to have a procedure that enabled us to be accountable and to monitor how the club stood financially. We now employ a part-time administrator who is responsible for keeping the club accounts and organising the payroll. This has been a great relief to all those on the staff who just want to get on with the business of looking after children."
Playworker in a well-established kids' club

CHAPTER **10**

Marketing your club

How to let everyone know just how good you are!

However you are funded, you will need to actively seek out and recruit. It might be that you are lucky and have a sufficient number of parents just waiting for the opportunity to use your club; it is more likely, however, that you will have to advertise your club in order to make sure your numbers build to the point where you will be able to break even.

Whichever scenario your club fits into, you will still need to keep parents and the local community properly informed about what you are doing and what is happening.

Stage 1

Consider who you want to reach and how to make information available to them. You may wish to target:

- the parents/guardians of children at your school;
- the parents of children at nearby schools;
- parents who work locally.

Stage 2

Look at each group you wish to target and determine how you might access them.

Parents/ guardians of children at your school

- newsletters from school
- prospectus
- report to parents from governors
- posters
- assemblies
- new parents' evening
- sports days and other events

Parents of children at neighbouring schools

- posters at the schools
- new parents' evenings
- leaflets

already had many of the items in place and that it wouldn't take us too long to brush up others. It certainly made us think carefully about our practice, and the visits from assessors provided us with very useful and positive feedback. We gained a level 2, which was more than we'd expected."

Coordinator of a primary school kids' club

Section 2
Club Practice

CHAPTER **12**

Activities in your club

Providing a balance of activities; the needs of different types of sessions

Clubs vary in how structured their activities are. Some clubs prefer to have organised activities in which all the attending children take part. Other clubs prefer to have something more flexible, with perhaps one organised activity but with children having the option of not taking part in this.

A lot will depend upon the ages of the children, how long they are there for, what kind of session it is and the strengths and number of staff on duty.

Make the most of seasonal events and activities. Smaller numbers and a higher adult/child ratio can sometimes mean you are able to engage in activities which would be more difficult to organise in the school day, e.g. making pancakes, craft and design projects.

You will need to treat before- and after-school and holiday times very differently in your approach to planning, as each has a different 'character' to it, i.e.

Before school

- There is insufficient time to organise children to do much productively.
- Breakfast can be a very good focus and take up most of the time.
- Have lots of construction items, board games and less energetic activities available in the lead up to school.

After school

- Children are often tired of being organised. Give them opportunities to relax, either through quiet activities or through more active pursuits such as outdoor games to get rid of their energy.
- Although there may be little time to 'make' something, if you do have a core of customers then something started one day can be continued on another. Do try to have at least one organised activity to provide stimulus and focus.

Holiday club

- Holiday time is when you will really need to plan a wide range of stimulating activities. You may wish to work to a theme each week and plan activities around this (e.g. 'space', animals, festivals, weddings, travel).
- Look at your plans in terms not only of across the week but also across the day. Have you built in time to relax after lunch? Do your activities at the end of the day allow for clearing up? What will happen if children arrive midway through a session?
- As the booking forms (Appendix O) arrive, look for busy periods and plan your main activities for then.
- Try to have a special event planned every week and publicise this specifically – you may get bored children whose parents do not need childcare wanting to take part too.
- As the club and numbers develop, try organising trips out. Initially these can just be to local places, e.g. the park or library. As you become more experienced, coach trips to more adventurous destinations can be organised.

Table 2: Activities checklist

	Holiday	Before school	After school
Art/craft activities	✓	✗	✓
Television/video	✓	✓	✓
Relaxation/quiet time e.g. reading	✓	✓	✓
Outdoor games	✓	✗	✓
Indoor board games	✓	✓	✓
Indoor games and circle activities	✓	✗	✓
Drama, role-play	✓	✓	✓
Treasure hunts, competitions	✓	✗	✓
Trips out	✓	✗	✗
Parties – special events	✓	✗	✓
Paper and pencil games and activities	✓	✓	✓
Cooking	✓	✗	✗

As you might expect from looking at the activities checklist in Table 2, a holiday club needs plenty of variety; a before-school club needs a less boisterous range of activities and an after-school club a mixture of the two, but with opportunities for children to 'let off steam' and/or relax.

It is important that you plan carefully and that the team collaborates, especially where different people work in different sessions. How you set out your planning is an important consideration, and there is a suggested planner in Appendix H of this book. Establishing a routine is important.

Activities should be set in the context of a clear framework of agreed procedures. There should be high expectations of children including at meal times. Some children may be spending a great deal of their out-of-school time in your charge. This places a heavy responsibility on the club to make sure that you are not just babysitting but are actively encouraging and developing children in an atmosphere of calm respect.

Across the week you should be aiming for a balance of activities. Although the club is not school, you should be aware of the children's developmental needs and should aim to provide them with as stimulating and varied an experience as possible.

Be aware of events happening in school and aim to incorporate or complement these without repetition or duplication. Theme weeks can be fun, and once children and parents are aware of the theme, they will sometimes offer their own suggestions and expertise. Some suggested themes include:

- the circus
- cartoon characters
- stories
- weddings
- Europe (or any continent and/or 'other cultures')
- hobbies
- carnival
- fashion
- pets

If you are able to supplement your activities with visits and visitors, this will add excitement to your week and will also make it very newsworthy for a local press release.

The acronym 'SPICE' is used to reflect the range that children should have available to them:

S Social development
P Physical development
I Imaginative development
C Cognitive development
E Emotional development

Extra-curricular clubs

There has recently been a drive towards establishing a greater diversity of after-school activities that incorporate school staff and have the aim of extending and developing areas of the curriculum out of school time.

You might be in a position to enable teachers and others to work peripatetically within your club, providing perhaps an hour of a specific activity. Clubs such as art, homework, gardening, sports, music etc. can be extremely enriching and add value to what you have to offer.

However, the aims of extra-curricular clubs are somewhat different. Out-of-school childcare must be available for several hours after school, and too intense an additional period of any activity may not be ideal for children who will also need some time to relax and unwind.

Traditionally, extra-curricular activities are free of charge when delivered by school staff. You might find some tension between children who are only there for the duration of the club and those who are paying because they are also within the care of the kids' club. These difficulties are not insurmountable, however, and it might be that children are exempt from paying for that period of time.

CHAPTER 14

Involving parents

Providing information, consultation and other points of contact

Several ways of involving and informing parents have already been covered in earlier chapters. Your parents should have been familiarised with procedures at the club through the supply of:

- introductory information for parents
- access to policy documents, e.g. child protection, behaviour management, health and safety
- regular newsletters

There should, however, be opportunities for parents to have a direct input into the working of the club. There should be an annual opportunity for parents to comment through:

- an annual general meeting
- a consultation questionnaire

Good practice should also enable parents to discuss informally their views and impressions about the club and allow them to feed through any comments they may have. It is useful to have a parents' noticeboard on which the next booking form, weekly plans and forthcoming events are displayed. Parents will appreciate details of staff and their qualifications being displayed, as well as the obligatory registration certificate and complaints procedure.

Try to involve parents in the life of the club as much as possible. A photograph album, with up-to-date photographs of the club at work and newspaper clippings, is useful to have on display in reception. Invite parents to parties and other special occasions. It will be appreciated if some of these are held in the evenings or at weekends.

You will need to consider how information relating to specific children should be communicated to parents and guardians, who will need to be informed of any accidents or incidents that have taken place while their children have been in your care. It is important that they sign acknowledgement of this information in your accident/incident book.

There may be other items of information, too, that can be usefully transferred. Club staff are sometimes in a position to observe behaviour and note social progress in a way that school staff are unable to. Small numbers, close proximity and involvement in a variety of practical and social activities can provide an illuminating environment for club staff. Indicators that might sometimes go unnoticed in other circumstances can be spotted in the 'family' atmosphere of a well-run club.

Do communicate anything you notice of interest. Clubs that are firmly based within the school are in a particularly good position to provide link information between home and school.

Chapter 17

Trips and events

Some guiding principles

Organised trips, especially during the long summer holiday, are always beneficial. But begin by planning short, local excursions to the library, park, shops or even another local kids' club.

Be aware that you will need to do the following:

- Leave at least two members of staff back in school for children who may arrive during the session or who are unable to go on the trip.
- Send out a parental consent form – (see Appendix P for an example of this).
- Make sure you have a first aider with you and a first aid kit, especially for longer excursions.
- Ask parents to supply suntan lotion prior to the trip if hot weather is likely.
- Give parents plenty of notice so they can budget and plan accordingly.
- Decide on a charging policy for your trips – if a coach or admission fee is involved you will have to charge for this in addition to your normal fee; this can be prohibitive for larger families and you may need to work out some special rates.
- Alternate between cheap and expensive trips, so making sure everyone has a chance to go out and that nobody is excluded on the basis of financial difficulty on a regular basis.
- Keep your staff-to-child ratio as low as possible; ask for volunteer parents and adults to come along, but remember that for any trip with significant periods of contact time with children (e.g. residential) they will need police checks.

Chapter 18

Maintaining your club, and the future

A list of routines to plan into your calendar

Once your school club routines are decided, your staff appointed and your club open and running successfully, the next stage for development is to ensure that the routines of maintaining the club are established clearly with as little emphasis upon school staff and management as possible. The aim is for an increased independence of your club while maintaining accountability and involvement.

Table 3 overleaf shows a list of routines with accompanying notes. Decide who will be responsible for doing what and absorb any that fall to you within your own weekly/ annual routines. There will still be some additional work but this should be kept to the minimum.

5. When would you use the club?

Before school ☐

After school ☐

Holiday periods ☐

6. How much would you be prepared to pay for this service?

£1.20 per hour ☐

£1.50 per hour ☐

Fixed charge £3.00 per day (term time) ☐

Please use this space to write down any other comments you may have:

Name: _____

Address: _____

_____

_____

Please tick this box if you would like us to keep you informed of any further developments: ☐

THANK YOU for taking the time to help us gather this important information. Please return the questionnaire to _____ at _____.

72

APPENDIX C

Sample club constitution

[*Name of club*] Management Committee

Constitution adopted on the .... day of ....

The [*Name of club*] will be administered according to this constitution by the members of the management committee.

Objectives

- To serve as a resource for local families by providing good quality affordable childcare.
- To foster an active partnership between parents, children and the school.
- To work with other agencies to provide the help and support needed.
- To employ and train members of the local community as playworkers.

Powers

In order to fulfil these objectives, the management committee may exercise the following powers:

- raise and apply for grants
- resource the centre
- employ staff
- make decisions relating to the future of the centre

Management committee

The management committee shall consist of at least one member from each of the following categories:

- Headteacher
- Governor
- Club coordinator
- Club playworker
- Local community representative
- Home/school liaison representative
- Club administrator

These shall be appointed by nomination.

APPENDIX E

Sample registration form

Registration Form for [*Name of club*] Club

_____ School

Child's details

Full Name:

Address:

Date of birth: Ethnic origin: Religion:

Name of
parent/guardian:

Parents' work
address:

Telephone Nos.   Evening: Daytime:

Details of second contact who may be contacted in an emergency:

Name:

Address:

Tel:

Name of person collecting the child:	

Details of child's doctor:

Name:	

Address:	

Tel:	

Child's medical history

Does your child have:

Details/further information

Any known allergies	Yes/No	
Asthma	Yes/No	
Diabetes	Yes/No	
Epilepsy	Yes/No	
Hearing problems	Yes/No	
Visual problems	Yes/No	
Hay fever	Yes/No	
Any other medical problem	Yes/No	
Is your child currently taking any form of medication?	Yes/No	

Please record any major infections or childhood illnesses your child has had:

Appendix F

Introductory information for parents

WELCOME to our school club. We hope you and your child will enjoy and benefit from our out-of-school provision. We aim to provide safe, enjoyable childcare within our school setting but without the timetable.

THIS LEAFLET contains information about [*Name of club*] Club. Please read it carefully as it will tell you what to expect from our club and what we expect from you in return.

PLEASE ASK if you need further details about the club or wish to make a suggestion. We pride ourselves in responding to club users and will try our best to provide a service which suits all our needs.

OUR CLUB is registered with social services and we are a member of the _____ Forum.

Contents   **page**
Our aims
Opening times
Fees and other charges
Leaving and collecting your child
Activities
Refreshments
Code of conduct
How you can help (parental involvement)

Our aims

We aim:

- to provide out-of-school care for children between the ages of 4 and 11 in a caring, safe environment;
- to provide training and work opportunities for members of the local community through offering employment within the club;
- to enable parents to access work and training opportunities through the provision of low-cost childcare;
- to encourage children to mix with and take responsibility for children of different ages;
- to involve children in a broad variety of extra-curricular activities;
- to provide emergency respite and 'time-out' for children associated with _____ School as the need arises.

Opening times

We are open:

Term time	8.00 – 9.00 a.m.
	3.30 – 6.00 p.m.
Holiday time	8.00 a.m. – 6.00 p.m. during the week

We are open every weekday except for bank holidays.

Fees and other charges:

Term time

8.00 – 9.00 a.m.	£1.20
3.30 – 4.30 p.m.	£1.60
4.30 – 5.30 p.m.	£1.50
5.30 – 6.00 p.m.	75p

During school holidays trips, visits and visitors might be booked which involve an extra charge. These events are usually subsidised by the club but will require

Holiday time

	Hour	Day (maximum)	Week (maximum)
Range A (first child)	£1.60	£15.00	£67.00
Range B (second child, first child for family on income support)	£1.60	£13.50	£60.00
Range C (charges for other children)	£1.60	£12.00	£50.00

an additional one-off payment. Events are optional and parents will be given plenty of notice where possible.

Children pay 25p towards the cost of breakfast and 50p for sandwiches at teatime. Drinks and biscuits are provided without extra charge.

We believe that having clear rules makes the club a more comfortable environment for everyone.

If children do not follow our code and/or break our rules we will:

1. Discuss their behaviour with them and explain the reasons for the rules;
2. Apply a school club sanction depending upon the nature of the behaviour and its repetition, including:

- removing a game/object
- referring to another playworker
- providing 'time-out'

Should inappropriate behaviour continue we will:

- inform parents and request their support;
- refer the child to the club coordinator using the school club referral book.

Should none of these approaches be successful, we reserve the right to ask parents to withdraw their child from the club. Obviously this would be a last resort, but we are sure you will agree that high standards and expectations are important if children in the club are to feel secure and safe.

How you can help

We recognise that our parents are very busy people! However, there are ways in which you can help support our club:

Let us know
If you have any ideas and/or suggestions for ways in which we can improve the club: we are always happy to hear your comments. If you have a problem or you are worried about some aspect of the club, please let one of our school club staff know. Alternatively, you can:

- speak to _____ in the school office;
- speak to _____ (the headteacher).

We will do our best to intercept problems at the earliest opportunity.

Resources
If you have any spare:

- paper, card, writing/colouring materials
- old (but intact) games, Lego, construction equipment, etc.

- dressing-up clothes
- old magazines, comics

. . . then please let us know.

Talents and skills

If you can contribute in any way to the activities offered in our club, we would like to know. You might be a skilful storyteller or story reader, or you might be good at painting or woodwork or have a similar skill. If you could donate an hour of your time to share your expertise we would be very grateful.

If you have any further questions about the club please ask. _____ or one of our playworkers will be happy to help you.

WE LOOK FORWARD TO YOUR CHILD JOINING US AND HOPE THAT THEY ENJOY THEIR OUT-OF-SCHOOL EXPERIENCE!

APPENDIX G

Business Plan for the period _____ to _____

Address of club:

Contact name and registration holder: _____

A before- and after-school and holiday club providing childcare for children between the ages of 4 and 11. A non-profit making organisation run by a management committee for the benefit of the local community.

Contract No: _____ (single regeneration budget)

Contents   page

Aims

- To provide out-of-school care for children attending _____
  School and within the local community in a caring, safe environment.
- To provide training and work opportunities for members of the local community.
- To encourage children to mix with children of different ages, from different schools and from different backgrounds.
- To involve children in a broad variety of extra-curricular activities.
- To provide emergency respite and 'time-out' for children associated with _____ School as the need arises.
- To extend and develop links with feeder infant schools to provide consistent childcare within the community.
- To extend and develop links with local secondary schools to provide continuity of provision.

Mission statement

We aim to provide good quality childcare in a supportive, secure environment, while addressing the needs of the families in the local community. Provision will be flexible and dependable and will acknowledge the difficult circumstances and fluctuating fortunes which many of our families experience.

Background information

_____ School lies at the heart of the _____ community. It caters for a rich cross-section of children, many of whom are from ethnic minority groups and some of whom belong to families facing personal difficulties. The area is characterised by the warmth of its community and the support which many families are prepared to give to local institutions and groups.

A questionnaire was distributed to parents and the results analysed. The response was positive. As a result, it was decided to go ahead with the club as soon as practicable. Two outside classrooms were vacant and ideal for use as an out-of-school club. Social services and the LEA were contacted and consulted about the club. A date was set and parents were informed.

It was planned to open the before- and after-school club in January _____ and extend this provision to a holiday club during February half-term.

A management committee was established (see Appendix B – Constitution). Staff were recruited, booking forms sent out and paperwork completed. On January 6th _____ the Mayor, _____, opened the club officially.

It has been noted that no other clubs currently exist in the immediate vicinity. Ideally, organisations within the local area should work together to provide a coherent, consistent range of childcare right through from birth to secondary school age. It is the intention of this club to help support such developments and possibly even contribute further to this. Pre-school provision and the transportation of children to and from infant schools are part of the club's plans.

About the club
Staffing

Current staffing levels are for two members of staff during each session to cater for a maximum of 16 children.

Current staff are:

_____ (playworker)
_____ (playworker)
_____ (playworker)
_____ (administrator)
_____ (coordinator)

Additional casual staff include:

_____ (casual playworker)
_____ (casual playworker)

We aim to provide staff with the relevant courses and training to help them develop their roles and skills. Priorities for staff training will include:

- first aid
- health and safety
- food handling – hygiene
- child protection
- equal opportunities
- playwork NVQ
- ideas for activities

Premises

The focus of our provision will be in the outside classrooms. These are two large vacant rooms which have access to the _____ entrance and include two toilets and one wash/hand basin. If we are to extend our numbers we will have to have an additional toilet and hand basin fitted in order to meet social services registration requirements.

In addition, there is a field area directly behind the classrooms and a large playground which can be used by the children. Food preparation will take place in the home studies room, which is also housed in an outside classroom close to the school club premises.

During holiday time, school facilities such as the home studies room and large halls will also be available for occasional use.

Fees

Fees are payable on a flexible basis according to the needs of parents. There is a sliding scale of charge which takes number of children and financial status into account.

Non-payment of fees will be followed up.

Term time   _____

Holiday time   _____

Admissions

Local children within the age range of 4–11 years are eligible to attend the '[*Name of club*] Club'. Priority will be given to those registering and attending first. All children will need a registration form filled in for them. During holiday times, those registering first will be saved a place. Once maximum numbers are reached, a waiting list of additional children will be made. If a booked place is not honoured, then:

- we will attempt to fill the place from children on the waiting list;
- if this is not possible, a charge will be made where reserved places are not honoured.

Booking forms for each subsequent holiday club will be made readily available through school-wide distribution and through placing in local feeder schools and in the club itself.

Refreshments

Light refreshments are provided during term time:

Breakfast:	toast and topping (25p)
	cereals
	juice

Tea:	sandwiches (50p)
	fruit
	light snacks
	juice

During cold weather, hot snacks will also be made available (e.g. soup and/or a warm drink).

During holiday time:

Breakfast:	toast and topping (25p)
	cereals
	juice

| Lunch: | packed lunch from home |
| | toast, hot soup, warm drink (to be available during cold weather) |

Breaks: toast and topping
juice
light refreshments

Activities

Staff take part in a weekly planning meeting during which a planning sheet is filled in for the following week. A balance of activities is aimed for, including:

- art/craft activities
- games – outdoor and indoor
- quiet activities – reading, jigsaws, colouring, use of construction equipment
- interactive activities – e.g. board games

Children are encouraged to mix across the age groups and to help and support one another. Older children are encouraged to take responsibility for younger children.

Children help with displays, and emphasis is placed upon ownership of the club and consultation. To help maintain the positive ethos of the club, each child has a 'congratulations card' on which they can collect stickers as a reward for particularly supportive, helpful behaviour. These are then accumulated until the card is completed, and children receive a certificate and a small reward.

As the club grows in size, it is intended to invite entertainers and organise club outings, especially during holiday periods.

Management group

The management committee consists of:

- Treasurer
- Chair
- Governor representative
- Community representative
- Playworkers

The committee meets once every half-term to discuss overall running of the club, future planning and strategies, and to review progress and financial information.

Playworkers meet weekly to decide on activities for subsequent weeks and to complete their planning sheets.

Communication and parental involvement

The club places a high priority upon involving parents and ensuring that parents are aware of developments and events. We are also keen to consult parents about their views and to collect suggestions to improve the facilities we offer. Ways in which we intend to do this include:

- half-termly newsletters distributed to all club attendees and all children at _____ School;
- a parents' noticeboard in the club entrance;
- bulletins in local papers and feeder schools;
- an annual questionnaires to parents;
- open days for parents to attend, observe and join in;
- making ourselves available for informal chats.

The Parent Information leaflet is aimed directly at new parents and includes information about the way the club is organised and what children and parents can expect. All registering parents receive one of these and sign their agreement to its procedures on the registration form.

Financial information

Cashflow forecast

SUMMARY	JAN	FEB	MAR	APR	MAY	JUN	JUL
Opening balance		-£4.00	-£442.00	-£346.00	-£664.00	-£322.00	-£586.00
Total receipts	£660.00	£60.00	£760.00	£180.00	£840.00	£400.00	£900.00
Total disbursements	£664.00	£496.00	£664.00	£498.00	£498.00	£664.00	£332.00
Total cash flow	-£4.00	-£438.00	£96.00	-£318.00	-£332.00	-£586.00	-£18.00
Ending balance	-£4.00	-£442.00	-£346.00	-£664.00	-£322.00	-£586.00	-£18.00

RECEIPTS							
Cash revenues	£60.00	£60.00	£160.00	£180.00	£240.00	£400.00	£300.00
Receivables							
Loans							
Other	£600.00		£600.00		£600.00		£600.00

DISBURSEMENTS							
Wages/salaries/	£624.00	£486.00	£624.00	£486.00	£486.00	£624.00	£312.00
Benefits							
Material							
Merchandise							
Equipment/vehicles, bought							
Equipment/vehicles, leased							
Advertising							
Supplies	£40.00	£30.00	£40.00	£30.00	£30.00	£40.00	£20.00

Figures based upon projected numbers of:

		January Budget	Actual	February Budget	Actual	March Budget	Actual
Income							
First hour	£1.60	£55.04		£69.00		£103.00	
Second hour	£1.50	£19.35		£32.25		£65.00	
TOTAL		£74.39		£101.25		£168.00	
Expenses							
Staffing	£112.50 p/w	£483.75		£483.75		£483.75	
Resources	£10.00 p/w	£43.00		£43.00		£43.00	
Premises	£30.00 p/w	£129.00		£129.00		£129.00	
TOTAL		£655.75		£655.75		£655.75	
Income – expenditure		-£581.36		-£554.50		-£487.75	

		April Budget	Actual	May Budget	Actual	June Budget	Actual
Income							
First hour	£1.60	£165.12		£206.00		£241.00	
Second hour	£1.50	£77.40		£96.75		£129.00	
TOTAL		£242.52		£302.75		£370.00	
Expenses							
Staffing	£112.50 p/w	£483.75		£483.75		£483.75	
Resources	£10.00 p/w	£43.00		£43.00		£43.00	
Premises	£30.00 p/w	£129.00		£129.00		£129.00	
TOTAL		£655.75		£655.75		£655.75	
Income – expenditure		-£413.23		-£353.00		-£285.75	

Holiday club cash flow forecast

SUMMARY	February	Easter	Spring	Summer	
Opening balance		-£330.50	-£399.50	-£417.00	£618.00
Total receipts	£220.00	£600.00	£450.00	£3,840.00	
Total disbursement	£550.00	£669.00	£467.50	£2,805.00	
Total cash flow	-£330.00	-£69.00	-£17.50	£1,035.00	
Ending balance	-£330.00	-£399.50	-£417.00	£618.00	£618.00

RECEIPTS					
Cash revenues	£220.00	£600.00	£450.00	£3,840.00	
Receivables					
Loans					
Others					

DISBURSEMENTS					
Wages/salaries/benefits	£500.00	£609.00	£417.50	£2,505.00	
Material					
Merchandise					
Equipment/vehicles, bought					
Equipment/vehicles, leased					
Advertising					
Supplies	£50.00	£60.00	£50.00	£300.00	
Services					
Maintenance/repairs					

_____ is club administrator. Procedures for collecting and recording money received include:

- recording dates when children are using the club;
- logging the monies received;
- weekly monitoring of monies received;
- logging of expenses incurred on production of receipts;
- banking of monies through Securicor collection.

The club operates its own payroll system which has been registered with HM Collector of Taxes in the _____ district. Employees are paid by cheque on a monthly basis.

Plans for the club _____ to _____

The priority for the club at present is to build numbers sufficiently to enable break-even to take place. In order to do this we must:

1. Publicise the club through:

- contacting local papers and radio stations
- displaying flyers in local shops
- contacting local feeder schools
- advertising within the school
- holding an open morning

2. Apply for additional grants, including:

- community education
- National Lottery
- Education Extra
- Children in Need

3. In addition we should:

- become involved in discussions relating to local childcare provision;
- develop and extend the activities we have on offer;
- ensure all staff have received appropriate training in health and safety, child protection, food handling, first aid and activity planning;
- register with appropriate groups;
- agree an equal opportunities policy;
- agree a health and safety policy;
- agree a child protection policy.

Long-term goals

1. Provide training for staff – enable staff to access appropriate childcare courses.
2. Build up our resources, including:

- television and video
- play and games equipment
- table tennis table
- table football
- computer
- minibus and garaging
- parachute

3. Improve our facilities by:

- adding two toilets and washbasins;
- carpets and curtains;
- improving access for wheelchairs;

- organising events and developing the breadth of activities available in the club.

_____ will see the review of this business plan and the policies outlined above.

Monthly targets

January	£25.00 per week
February	£35.00 per week
March	£50.00 per week
April	£75.00 per week
May	£100.00 per week
June	£125.00 per week
July	£175.00 per week

Appendix H

Weekly plans

Week beginning:

	Activity a.m.	Games a.m.	Activity p.m.	Games p.m.
Monday				
Tuesday				
Wednesday				
Thursday				
Friday				

Review of the week:

Notes on individuals:

APPENDIX 1

Handbook for staff

Contents   *page*

Introduction

Started in January _____, the [*Name of club*] is a facility aimed at parents of children at _____ School. It extends to parents in the local community, to whom the club is accessible.

It benefits from the availability of two outside classrooms which are ideally situated for a kids' club and enable easy access for parents. As a new venture, it is expected that the club will 'start small' and extend as parents begin to recognise the possibilities for themselves and their children.

Aims of the club

- To provide out-of-school care for children between the ages of 4 and 11 in a caring, safe environment.
- To provide training and work opportunities for members of the local community through offering employment within the club.
- To enable parents to access work and training opportunities through the provision of low-cost childcare.
- To encourage children to mix with and take responsibility for children of different ages.
- To involve children in a broad variety of extra-curricular activities.
- To provide emergency respite and 'time-out' for children associated with _____ school as the need arises.

Club Summary

How we work

We are open:

Term time   8.00 – 9.00 a.m.
                  3.30 – 6.00 p.m.

Holiday time   8.00 a.m. – 6.00 p.m. during the week

We are open every weekday except for bank holidays.

Fees and other charges:

Term time

8.00 – 9.00 a.m.	£1.60
3.30 – 4.30 p.m.	£1.60
4.30 – 5.30 p.m.	£1.50
5.30 – 6.00 p.m.	75p

Holiday time

	Hour	Day (maximum)	Week (maximum)
Range A (first child)	£1.60	£15.00	£67.00
Range B (second child, first child for family on income support)	£1.60	£13.50	£60.00
Range C (charges for other children)	£1.60	£12.00	£50.00

During school holidays, trips, visits and visitors might be booked which involve an extra charge. These events are usually subsidised by the club but will require an additional one-off payment. Events are optional and parents will be given plenty of notice where possible.

Children pay 25p towards the cost of breakfast and 50p for sandwiches at teatime. Drinks and biscuits are provided without extra charge.

Food Preparation

Basic guidelines include:

- non-meat products only to be used in sandwiches;
- breakfasts to be prepared using cereals/toast in the school club;
- sandwiches and other items to be prepared in the Home Economics room;
- perishable items to be stored in the fridge in the Home Economics room.

Refreshments

Before school   *Breakfast (25p)*
drinks
toast
cereal

After school   *Refreshments (no charge)*
drinks and biscuits

Tea (50p)
sandwiches
fruit
toast

Holidays   *Lunch*
Children will need to bring a packed lunch

Club staff must ensure that dietary requirements identified by parents on registration forms are followed.

Staff noticeboard

This should be updated weekly to include:

- a copy of the latest planning sheet;
- information about courses;
- examples of the next holiday booking form.

Parents' noticeboard

This should include:
- information to pass on immediately, e.g. if a child has had a minor accident, or if there is information from school that needs to be relayed;
- information about future bookings and events;
- a copy of the latest newsletter.

Information for parents

Newsletters are produced by the club coordinator every half-term. These include information about:

- staffing
- resources
- trips and events
- children's comments
- requests

Booking forms are issued during each holiday for the next holiday period.

On registering any new child, parents/guardians must:

- complete the registration form;
- receive and sign a copy of the 'Information for Parents' document.

Health and safety

A fire practice is held once every term and once during Easter and summer holidays. Children are assembled on the grass while the register is taken, and then may return to the building once the 'all clear' is given. One playworker is responsible for calling the fire brigade and one for staying with the children.

Whenever a significant incident or accident occurs, a note should be made in the accident book and parents should be informed when collecting their child. All playworkers should be familiar with the child's registration form and have their attention drawn to any significant medical difficulties and/or issues of consent that may be applicable.

Medicines should be kept securely and logged in the medicines book. Inhalers should be easily accessible for the children but should also be logged.

The club coordinator is the person with responsibility for child protection. Any concerns relating to the health and safety of individual children should be reported to the coordinator.

Staff should be vigilant in terms of their gender and that of the children. Male members of staff, in particular, should not accompany girls on their own to the toilet. Injuries of a 'delicate' nature should be dealt with by a member of staff of the same sex as the patient.

Equal opportunities

It is extremely important that all members of staff:

- encourage children to try a variety of activities irrespective of gender;
- order resources which reflect the cultural backgrounds of the children;
- plan activities which celebrate the religious and cultural diversity of the club;
- recognise a variety of key religious celebrations;
- encourage children to mix and support one another;
- take a firm line on any form of discrimination, including sexism or racism;
- avoid stereotypical language (e.g. 'boys are naughty', 'what a pretty girl', 'when your mother does the washing up', etc.).

Staff training

It is a priority of the club that staff should receive the training they need. Emphasis is placed upon:

- first aid courses
- health and safety courses
- food hygiene courses
- child protection courses
- NVQ playcare qualifications
- ideas for activities

Roles and responsibilities
Club coordinator

- Produce half-termly newsletters.
- Maintain overview of the club.
- Support the behaviour policy.
- Attend management committee meetings.
- Liaise with social services and other organisations.
- Apply for grants and other sources of funding.

Club administrator's duties

- Maintain cashflow records.
- Oversee the ordering of resources.
- Maintain personnel records and payroll.
- Help maintain records of payment.

Playworkers' responsibilities

- Ensure parents sign children in and out.
- Maintain day-to-day records of money received.
- Register children.
- Make use of ten-minute preparation time to collect and organise resources.
- Make use of ten-minute clearaway time to ensure club is left safe and tidy.
- Meet weekly to plan activities, completing planning sheet.
- Meet half-termly with the management committee to discuss the overall progress of the club.
- Be welcoming to parents and ensure that necessary information is passed across.
- Be involved actively with the children.
- Be mindful of safety issues, ensuring that children are only collected by those agreed.
- Attend to hygiene during food preparation and be aware of dietary needs of children.
- Keep updated on first aid.
- Be prepared to receive further training.

The role of the management committee

- Meet half-termly to oversee the club's progress.
- Review cashflow and make decisions related to this.
- Make strategic decisions about the club's future.

Planning activities

We aim to involve children in a range of activities, while allowing them the freedom to make choices and relax. During the week organised activities should include:

- art/craft activities
- sports/games – indoor and outdoor, depending on the weather
- quiet activities (e.g. reading, jigsaws, colouring, use of construction equipment)
- interactive activities (e.g. board games)
- role play

Children will also be encouraged to do their homework during after-school club.

Activities should be planned during the weekly staff meeting, filled in on the weekly planner and kept in the planning folder. Staff are responsible for collecting the resources together for this. Where a particular activity will require additional resources, these must be ordered well in advance.

During holidays, a theme should be planned for each week. This should include at least one 'fun day' during which an organised trip takes place and/or some other kind of special event.

During spring and summer, the club's outdoor activities should be prevalent, and should make good use of the school grounds and playground. Children might also be taken on to the school field for games. Where this is the case:

- Children must not cross the road to return to school unattended.
- Children must not be left unsupervised on the field.

In some cases, facilities within the main school building can be used.

Display

The displays in classrooms used by the club are the responsibility of the club. It is important to display children's work and encourage parents to see what they have produced. Boards should be backed and work should be mounted appropriately; 3-D displays are particularly welcome. Children's names should be displayed next to their work. Older children might actively be encouraged to take part in the production of the display.

Termly newsletters update parents on past and planned trips and events and provide information about holiday club themes.

Procedure 1: Before school

Club staff should be ready to receive children by 7.55 a.m. Children may arrive at the club at 8.00 a.m. They should be welcomed by one member of staff, signed in by parent/guardian and coats and bags hung in the reception area.

Children may then have breakfast and/or take part in a settled morning activity. A choice should be available.

At 8.45 a.m. children should help playworkers to clear away after the morning session. They should collect their bags and coats and be released into the playground to line up with the other children as the bell is rung.

In some cases it may be necessary for the playworker to see the child's class teacher if there is a particular message to convey.

Procedure 2: After school

Activities should be prepared and ready for children once school is over. There should be available:

1. A quiet room which will be used initially for homework/reading/art/craft activities.
2. A tea/games room (initially refreshments will be set up in here).

As children arrive, they should:

- hang up their bags and coats in the reception area;
- be marked on the register;
- help themselves to refreshments/tea – sitting down to eat.

All children must be seated when eating and good table manners should be encouraged. This should be a peaceful, communal time when stories from the day might be shared and children generally encouraged to discuss what they have been doing. As children finish eating, they should be taken into the quiet room by one playworker, who should:

- explain the range of activities available to them;
- encourage children to complete homework tasks.

Children will then choose an activity. Only when they have indicated their choice, should they be allowed to go. Children may later swap activities, but must be encouraged to pursue their original choice for a reasonable length of time.

As children are discussing the activities in the quiet room, the second playworker should tidy up the refreshments and prepare games/construction items in the 'active room'. On occasion it might be that a group game is organised in here that requires furniture to be moved back.

As parents arrive to collect their children they should:

- be welcomed and sign their child out;
- be informed of any particular incident that has occurred.

Procedure 3: Holiday club

During holiday time it is important that planning takes account of the fact that children may be spending a large amount of time at the club. Activities should be varied and balanced and allow for the needs both of children who are full time and those who are using the club less frequently.

When the weather is fine, outside facilities should be used. There should also be two additional break times during the day when children are gathered together for a drink and toast/biscuits. At this point, all activity should stop and children should be encouraged to reflect on what they have done so far and what they propose to do next.

After lunch, a quiet time should be organised with a short video/TV programme or story time in which food is allowed to settle. Parents should be informed of activities in the club on a daily basis through the parents' noticeboard.

On one day a 'fun day' should be organised. This should incorporate a special event such as a barbecue/disco/party, a visiting entertainer or a visit outside school. Parents can be invited to this event.

APPENDIX J

Behaviour policy

We expect a high standard of behaviour in our club. Children are encouraged to be:

- polite
- supportive of one another
- cooperative and respectful to members of staff
- attentive to the needs of others
- responsible towards their environment

We do have some specific rules:

- Children must walk in the school building.
- Children must share equipment and play fairly.
- Children must clear up after themselves and return items they have borrowed.
- Children must do as they are asked by a member of staff.

We believe that having clear rules makes the club a more comfortable environment for everyone.

If children do not follow our code and/or break our rules we will:

1. Discuss their behaviour with them and explain the reasons for the rules.
2. Apply a school club sanction, dependent upon the nature of the behaviour and its repetition, including:

- removal of a game/object;
- referral to another playworker;
- provision of 'time-out'.

Should inappropriate behaviour continue we will:

- inform parents and request their support;
- refer the child to the club coordinator using the school club referral book.

Should none of these approaches be successful, we reserve the right to ask parents to withdraw their child from the club.

It is important that staff are:

- consistent

- fair
- calm
- positive

A positive approach using rewards is an essential feature of the behaviour policy. Each child attending the club has a 'Congratulations card' which is used to reward children for helpful behaviour and supporting one another.

They should be given a sticker to place on their card. When the card is full the child is given a certificate in school assembly and reward from the school club 'goody bucket'.

Children must be clear about the club's approach. During the first session they spend with the club they should have explained to them:

- the rules and why we have them;
- what will happen if they are broken;
- the kinds of behaviour we expect to see;
- what the rewards for this behaviour will be.

Working with parents

Parents are involved in the [*Name of club*] club through:

- the issue of questionnaires – canvassing opinion on an annual basis;
- regular information via newsletters;
- invitations to open days and trips/events.

Parents should be informed on collection where there has been an incident/ accident in the club. The parents' noticeboard should include details of any information to pass on. Early discussion with parents where there is a possible difficulty should always be encouraged.
There may be opportunities for parents to offer particular skills in the club. This should be encouraged. Contributions of materials, expertise and unwanted items can be requested.

Timetable for planning

Weekly

- staff planning meetings

Half-termly

- management committee meetings
- newsletter issue
- production of booking form for next holiday club

Annually

- staff development meetings
- review of policies
- review of business plan
- parent consultation questionnaires

APPENDIX K

Health and safety policy

All club staff will have a copy of this policy and be required to implement it.

Contents   *page*

The role of the school management
The role of the club coordinator
The role of school club workers
School club safety rules – for children, staff and parents
Procedure for accident reports
Procedure for incident reports
Checking equipment
Monitoring implementation

The role of the school management

The headteacher, in conjunction with the governing body, is the officer initially and ultimately responsible for achieving the objectives of this health and safety policy. This responsibility includes liaison with the club coordinator in respect of:

- health and safety issues directly relevant to the club;
- equipment used by the school club;
- premises used by the club;
- food preparation and storage;
- training needs and monitoring of staff;
- health and safety procedure and policy implementation.

The role of the club coordinator

Under the direction of the headteacher, the coordinator is responsible for implementing the health and safety policy objectives which are within his/her direct control. As part of additional supervisory responsibility the coordinator should:

1. Ensure that all club staff are familiar with this health and safety policy and that they fulfil their own responsibilities.
2. Ensure that any health and safety matter brought to their attention receives prompt and appropriate action. This might include dealing appropriately with an incident, recording the incident, consulting with the headteacher, seeking further advice or liaison with parents or site service staff.
3. Design and implement a programme for health and safety which includes:

- accident prevention
- procedure for recording and reporting incidents
- procedures for identifying, reporting and reducing hazards

4. Ensure the provision of training for those employees without the necessary health and safety experience.

5. Ensure that screening of new employees takes place.

6. Keep the headteacher informed about any major incidents or health and safety issues arising from club work.

7. Keep under constant review the effectiveness of the site's policy and bring to the attention of the headteacher any changes which may be thought necessary.

8. Ensure that adequate and appropriate equipment is available for use in the club and that it is maintained to a safe standard.

9. Ensure that the advice of the specialist support services is sought on any health and safety mater for which clarification or assistance is required.

10. Show proper concern for the health and safety of students and visitors and bring to their attention the need to take reasonable care of themselves and other persons who may be affected by their acts.

The role of the club worker

It is the responsibility of the playworker to:

- report any hazard or piece of broken/dangerous equipment to the coordinator;
- record details of any hazardous or dangerous equipment and/or any breakages which may occur;
- follow all policy recommendation, procedures and programmes;
- take responsible care for the health and safety of him/herself and other persons who may be affected by his/her acts;
- maintain equipment in good condition and report any accidents or breakages to the coordinator;
- report all accidents to the coordinator and the child's parent or guardian;
- record accidents in the accident book;
- record any significant incidents or chastisements at the back of the accident book;
- attend health and safety training courses as required;
- be aware of the evacuation and provision procedures and of the position of the fire alarms and equipment;
- take the children through a termly fire drill practice (children are to assemble on the grassed area in front of the school building for register call);
- have access to emergency numbers for contacting parents/guardians, headteacher, social services and club coordinator;
- ensure that the highest standards of hygiene are maintained in any matter referring to food and drink.

Safety rules

These rules should be discussed and shared with children.

Children should:

- walk between play areas and activities;
- be seated while eating and at meal times;
- be responsible for clearing up activities once they have finished playing;
- be supervised in the playground and on the playing field;
- be encouraged to be aware of the safety of themselves and others while at play;
- always be signed in and out of morning and afternoon club respectively;
- be collected only by an agreed adult.

Accidents procedure

In the event of an accident occurring during a school club session, the following procedure should be followed:

1. Immediate action taken within health and safety guidelines to remedy the effects of the accident.
2. Seeking of further advice or support as deemed necessary.
3. Recording of the accident in the accident book. Information entered in the book should include:

- date
- time
- nature of accident
- people involved
- action taken
- people informed

4. Liaison following the accident with parents or guardians and the club coordinator.
5. Consideration of the cause of the accident and ways in which it might have been prevented.

Incident procedure

In the event of an incident occurring during a school club session, the following procedure should be followed:

1. Immediate action taken within health and safety guidelines to remedy or deal with the incident.
2. Seeking further advice or support as deemed necessary.
3. Recording of the incident in the incident section of the accident book. This should include:

- date
- time
- nature of incident
- people involved
- action taken
- people informed

4. Liaison following the incident with parents or guardians and club coordinator.
5. Reflection on the incident and consideration of ways in which it might have been avoided.

Procedures for late collection and behaviour concerns are outlined in the school club policies and procedures document.

Equipment maintenance

Any damage, breakage, loss or area of concern should be reported to the club coordinator.

It is important that all equipment obtained is checked before use in the club by the club administrator. It should be:

- appropriate for the age range;
- in accordance with British Safety Standards;
- in good working order;
- safe for use with children.

Resources should be in line with the equal opportunities policy.

Monitoring implementation

The club coordinator will monitor implementation of this policy through a bi-annual check to include:

- the accident book
- the incident book
- children's awareness of club rules and safety

There will also be bi-annual discussion with school club staff as part of the formal meeting process concerning health and safety issues. It will be expected that matters concerning health and safety will be raised as a constant agenda item, both formally and informally.

APPENDIX **L**

Equal opportunities policy

Aims and objectives

- To conduct our school club in a way which positively asserts people's rights to equality of consideration and opportunity.
- To provide children with a variety of adult role models.
- To ensure equal opportunities for club staff to develop their potential.
- To offer training and staff development for individuals working for the club.
- To recruit new staff, following correct procedures as outlined in the school's and authority's equal opportunities guidelines.
- To ensure that the contributions of all staff are recognised and valued.
- To provide support for adults associated with the club to progress and take up further appointments.
- To encourage children in the club to recognise their own value and the value of others.
- To recognise the importance of the home environment and develop links which provide a supportive experience for children between the school day and their home life.
- To monitor and purchase equipment with concern for representation of different groups.
- To encourage children to sample from a variety of different activities irrespective of gender/ethnic/cultural group.
- To respect dietary requirements and preferences associated with different groups.
- To draw attention to and discuss stereotyping and bias when unavoidably encountered.
- To include specific activities which reflect the variety of cultures and groups represented within the school and in society generally.
- To monitor language used for stereotypical remarks and preconceptions.
- To challenge any overtly racist/sexist remark.

- To ensure that children have access to all resources.
- To label displays in more than one language.
- To check that equal time is given to different groups and genders.
- To ensure that children are encouraged to take part in a variety of different activities.

Staff development

The school club is an ideal opportunity for individuals to re-enter the jobs market and polish or extend their experience and qualifications. The development of staff should be a key feature of club ethos and should be achieved through:

- annual development meetings identifying training and development needs;
- the prioritising of training for club workers;
- the nurturing of an ethos of encouragement and positive feedback;
- the raising of individual self-esteem;
- the provision of childcare facilities for those working within the club;
- flexibility for club workers which enables them to take up the full range of opportunities available to them;
- the provision of references and support for the continued development of staff outside the immediate organisation;
- continued career advice and support.

In order for the club to provide a welcoming atmosphere and opportunities for all social groups, it is important that members of staff are:

- familiar with this policy;
- able to discuss issues and understand their implications;
- encouraged to attend equal opportunities courses.

In order that children see a variety of adult role models in the full range of positions and levels of responsibilities, it is important that:

- care is taken to uphold the LEA guidance on advertisement and appointment procedure;
- staff are encouraged to extend and vary their roles within the club;
- staff adopt and encourage a variety of different types of activity;
- the full range of community groups is represented within the staff team as far as is possible.

Activities

It is important that all children using the club have access to and are encouraged to explore, experiment with and experience a full range of materials, resources and activities. In order to fulfil this obligation, school club workers should:

- encourage children to select from a wide variety of activities;
- be careful not to prejudge the type of activity which children might choose;
- be supportive of any child choosing an activity not normally associated with their gender;
- provide 'openings' for more reticent children to take part in highly popular activities and prevent monopolising of equipment and space;
- report on and discuss any difficulties or imbalances which they have noted.

In using resources, children should see their own community group represented and catered for. This should be achieved through:

- the careful ordering of resources to reflect multicultural Britain;
- seeking advice and involvement of individuals from a variety of community groups in planning and organising activities;
- celebration of different religious festivals.

Admissions

Access to the school club should be made as broad as possible in order to benefit those most needing the facility. In order to further this intention it is important that:

- publicity is extensive and reaches a varied audience;
- fees are kept as low as possible;
- exclusion of any child from the club remains a last resort;
- all children receive a warm welcome;
- in setting fees, allowance is made for some aspects of family circumstances.

This might be further developed in future by:

- greater subsidy of places for low-income families;
- some temporary emergency places made available for children in need.

Our registration document requests dietary and medical information, which enables special consideration to be given to individuals with alternative dietary requirements from our standard ones.

Children will be admitted to the club in emergency situations.

Resources

The school club has a responsibility to make sure that the resources it uses reflect the cultural diversity of the community it serves. In order to ensure that this takes place it is important that:

- all new resources are checked for examples of bias and stereotyping;
- resources are selected to provide role-model examples;
- materials are bought to support a multicultural range of activities;
- any resource books purchased provide a range of activity suggestions.

Management

It is the responsibility of the school club term-time and holiday coordinators to monitor the success of this policy and to ensure that the recommendations included here are part of the whole school club approach. It is important that:

- coordinators encourage and support the development of a welcoming and stimulating environment for all children;
- behaviour of children is conducive to this and inappropriate language is quickly and firmly dealt with;
- coordinators conduct a regular review of the policy;
- coordinators take notice of the level to which the club satisfies community needs.

Behaviour of children

It is vital that any antisocial, racist or sexist behaviour and/or language is challenged immediately and that children are aware that such attitudes will not be tolerated in the club. This includes children who:

- use offensive language towards one another;
- display a hostile/aggressive attitude to other children;
- openly express views which could be upsetting to others.

Where this occurs, staff should:

- make the unacceptability of this behaviour known to all those witnessing the incident;
- take the offender aside and clearly explain that this is not acceptable and why;
- ensure that any child affected by the behaviour or language is also taken

aside, their reaction discussed and positive support provided;
- encourage both parties to overcome the incident and seek apologies or explanations where appropriate.

If the club worker is in any doubt about any long-term effects which the incident might have, or feels that matters remain unresolved, they should refer the incident to the club coordinator for further attention.

Monitoring and evaluation

This policy will have been successful if:

- all children attending the club feel equally welcome and comfortable there, irrespective of background/culture/gender;
- incidents are efficiently and effectively dealt with to prevent any recurrence;
- the activities and resources on offer reflect the diversity of children in the local community;
- club workers reflect the diversity of the local community;
- staff have the opportunity to develop and pursue their own development needs;
- children select a variety of activities and are prepared to experiment with new ones.

It is the responsibility of all club workers to implement this policy on a day-to-day basis.

It is the responsibility of the club coordinator to familiarise staff with this policy. He/she should also monitor its effectiveness and keep it up to date by reviewing it on an annual basis.

APPENDIX M

Job descriptions

Job description for the post of holiday club coordinator:

Purpose of the job

- To help create a safe, caring and interesting environment for children attending the [*Name of club*] Club during the holidays.
- To coordinate the day-to-day organisation of the club and support playworkers.

General duties and responsibilities

- To plan, prepare and clear away play activities.
- To participate actively with the children.
- To help maintain records, including registers, registration forms, accident books, weekly plans and financial records.
- To help maintain display boards.
- To build good relationships with the children within a calm, disciplined but stimulating environment.
- To liaise with parents, other club workers and school staff.
- To meet with other holiday club staff prior to the opening of the club.
- To help maintain and monitor equipment.
- To help prepare refreshments.
- To follow procedures as indicated in the club's procedure documents, including health and safety and child protection.
- To be familiar with and act upon the school's equal opportunities policy.
- To review the success of the club.

Additional coordinating duties

- To be responsible for advertising the club.
- To be responsible for ensuring that school premises are secure at the end of the day and to open up where appropriate.
- To coordinate the planning of activities around a theme.
- To organise an 'open-day' and/or event.
- To be responsible for the staffing rota during the holiday club.
- To provide a report at the end of the club for discussion at the management committee meeting.
- To manage and lead the team of playworkers.

Responsible to:

The school club management committee

Our commitment:

- Annual professional development meetings and guidance.
- Training and skill development where funds allow.

Job description for the post of school club worker:

Purpose of the job

- To help create a safe, caring and interesting environment for children attending the [*Name of club*] Club during school club opening times.
- To play a key role in organising and leading sporting activities.
- To assist in the day-to-day organisation of the out-of-school club.

General duties and responsibilities

- To plan, prepare and clear away play activities.
- To participate actively with the children.
- To help maintain records, including registers, registration forms, accident books, weekly and termly plans and financial records.
- To help maintain display boards.
- To build good relationships with the children within a calm, disciplined but stimulating environment.
- To liaise with parents, other club workers and school staff.
- To meet half-termly to review and plan activities in conjunction with members of the management committee.
- To help maintain and monitor equipment.
- To help prepare refreshments.
- To follow procedures as indicated in the club's procedure documents, including health and safety and child protection.
- To be familiar with and act upon the school's equal opportunities policy.
- To plan with other playworkers on a weekly basis.
- To attend courses and training as provided by the club.

Specific duties

- To help lead children in sporting activities.

Responsible to:

The school club management committee

Our commitment:

- Annual professional development meetings and guidance.
- Training and skill development where funds allow.

Child protection guidelines

Contents   **page**

Rationale
Responsibilities for playworkers
Actions for playworkers
Agencies to contact
Keeping records
Code of conduct
Monitoring and evaluation

Rationale

A kids' club has a unique role in the life of child and parent. The relationships built between playworkers and families should be a mixture of respect and familiarity. Some children will spend almost as much time in out-of-school care as in school, and certainly more than they do at home. The special relationships which develop can sometimes result in playworkers being confided in, relied upon for advice and involved in discussions about the welfare of the children they cater for.

In most cases, the relationships and knowledge gained will fit well within the caring role of the playworker. In some, however, problems may arise, and playworkers may be witness to signs of abuse which have remained undisclosed to other agencies. It is in such cases that these protection procedures should be administered.

".. the possibility of workers being made aware of physical, sexual or emotional abuse is high."
(KCN 'School's Out')

Responsibilities for playworkers

It is the responsibility of every school club playworker to remain:

- vigilant for evidence of abuse;
- alert to signs of unusual behaviour and/or changes in behaviour;
- sensitive to the needs of individual children;
- aware of aspects of family history which may affect the child's behaviour or needs;

- aware of being placed in situations which may leave themselves open to allegations.

School club playworkers should aim to:

- build constructive relationships with individual children based on mutual respect;
- establish welcoming relationships with parents in a spirit of partnership.

Actions for playworkers

A school club worker who is concerned in any way about an individual child should:

- reassure the child that they are safe/have done the right thing;
- look after the immediate needs of the child in terms of comfort and/or safety;
- look for support from another playworker where appropriate;
- make their concern known to the club coordinator and/or headteacher;
- if the above persons are not immediately available, judge the urgency of the situation and consult with the necessary authority in cases of emergency.

Playworkers should not promise children confidentiality. They should always proceed with caution, placing the safety and welfare of the child as the priority. They should be cautious as to putting themselves at risk and other children within the club.

Agencies to contact

Agencies/individuals who may be contacted in cases of emergency or for advice include:

- social services department
- school nurse
- NSPCC Child Protection Team
- local police officer

"A playcare worker's responsibilities do not include investigating the suspected abuse. However, playcare workers should keep accurate records of their observations and of anything said to them by the child or others in connection with the suspected abuse. It is always important to listen to children."

(KCN 'Procedures for suspected child abuse')

Keeping records

Where abuse is suspected, a record should be kept of:

- what was observed, when and by whom;
- any injury, with a written description or drawing as appropriate;
- comments made by the child and/or others involved;
- any explanation given by the adult/child of how the injury happened;
- any subsequent action, referral or response;
- any review date agreed or further consultation needed.

Code of conduct

Parents should be involved and informed at every stage, except in cases of suspected sexual abuse or where the safety of any individual may be threatened.

Do not make promises of confidentiality.

Reassure adults and children who have reported abuse that they have done the right thing by telling someone.

All disclosures of abuse must be taken seriously.

Record, take advice and report when you have a concern. Don't wait until it's too late.

Issues and allegations of staff misconduct should also be taken seriously and investigated.

Monitoring and evaluation

The effectiveness and appropriateness of these procedures should be reviewed annually. Each incident causing concern over the previous year should be reviewed and reconsidered.

Appendix O

Booking forms

[*Name of club*] KIDS' CLUB

OCTOBER HOLIDAY CLUB

OPEN 8.00 a.m. – 6.00 p.m.

Monday October 26th – Friday 30th October

Names of child(ren)	Age	Class/school

I have/have not already completed a registration form.

Holiday Booking Form		
	A.M.	P.M.
Monday 26th October		
Tuesday 27th October		
Wednesday 28th October		
Thursday 29th October		
Friday 30th October		

Please indicate the time children will be attending e.g. 8.00 – 6.00; 8.00 – 12.00

Signed:_____ Date:_____

(Please note – we need accurate numbers to help us plan our club. Please do not book your children in unless you will definitely take up the places. If you are unsure, could you please write this on the booking form)

APPENDIX P

Permission slip

[*Name of club*] Kids' Club Easter outing to _____

Trip leader:

Named first aider:

Departure time:

Return time:

Required to take:

Pocket money:

Cost:

There will be a ratio of one adult to four children arranged in groups of 10 children, with one member of staff plus two volunteer helpers. All staff have first aid certificates.

Groups will be arranged before departing, and children should know their group leaders so that they can listen to instructions concerning the day trip and give any valuables to the group leaders (e.g. pocket money) for safekeeping.

The trip leader will be in contact with the club at various times throughout the trip.

PERMISSION SLIP

For _____

To go to _____ on _____

Signed _____ Date _____

Contact number of parent/carer during the trip _____

Appendix Q

Staff development information

Name:

Address:

Job description:

General duties and responsibilities
- To plan, prepare and clear away play activities.
- To participate actively with the children.
- To help maintain records, including registers, registration forms, accident books, weekly and termly plans and financial records.
- To help maintain display boards.
- To build good relationships with the children within a calm, disciplined but stimulating environment.
- To liaise with parents, other club workers and school staff.
- To meet half-termly to review and plan activities in conjunction with the club coordinator.
- To help maintain and monitor equipment.
- To follow procedures as indicated in the club's procedure document, including health and safety, equal opportunities and child protection.

CV checklist

Area	Details	Date
First Aid		
Police check		
Childcare qualifications		
Childcare experience		
Other qualifications/experience		
Present and future development	**Details**	**Date**
Current courses		
Identified training needs		
Links with club objectives		
Suggestions for future development		

Signed _____
(playworker)

Signed _____
(appraiser)

APPENDIX R

Useful contacts

You will need to find out the contact names and numbers in your local area for:

- Day Care Adviser
- Environmental Health Offices
- Health Promotion Department
- Social Services Children's Team

National Childminders' Association
8 Masons Hill, Bromley, Kent
Tel: 020 8464 6164

National Children's Bureau
8 Wakley Street, London EC1V 7QE
Tel: 020 7843 6000

Pre-School Learning Alliance
61-63 Kings Cross Road, London WC1X 9LL
Tel: 020 7833 0991

Kids' Club Network (after-school care)
Belleive house, 3 Mirfield Crescent, London E14 9SZ
Tel: 020 7512 2112

Education Extra
17 Old Ford Road London E2 9PL
Tel: 020 8709 9900